D1353301

TWENTY FIVE YEARS OF
LONDON TRANSPORT
1949-1974

Kevin McCormack

Ian Allan
PUBLISHING

First published 2014

ISBN 978 0 7110 3699 4

© Kevin McCormack 2014

Published by Ian Allan Publishing Ltd, Hersham, Surrey, KT12 4RG.

Printed in China

Visit the Ian Allan Publishing website at *www.ianallanpublishing.com*

FRONT COVER Pride of the LT trolleybus fleet were the post-war, 8ft-wide Q1 class totalling 127 vehicles, all but two of which were sold to Spanish operators in 1961. In the previous year, Nos 1779 and 1831 from Isleworth depot stand at the Hounslow terminus of route 657 in Staines Road, near the junction with Wellington Road. *Marcus Eavis/Online Transport Archive*

TITLE PAGE Three members of BEA's 65-strong fleet of forward-entrance Routemasters with luggage trailers rest at Heathrow Airport in July 1969, awaiting their next journey on the LT-operated service to the West London Air Terminal at Gloucester Road. *Marcus Eavis/Online Transport Archive*

REAR COVER The difference between the 1923 G stock motor cars and later clerestory roof stock with rounded ends is clearly evident in this view at Acton Town in May 1955. No 4167, on the right, was one of two such cars fitted with a second driving cab in 1939 for use on the single-car shuttle service to South Acton which was withdrawn on 28 February 1959. *Raymond DeGroote/Online Transport Archive*

Introduction

Following the success of my first London Transport colour album to combine road and rail operations, *London Transport in Colour 1950-1969* published in 2005, the format is being repeated in this new album covering a 25-year span from 1949 to 1974. Once again, every effort has been made to find previously unpublished colour images to illustrate that much-loved undertaking, London Transport ("LT").

Although there are a few photographs taken at either end of the time line, I make no apology for the fact that the majority of the material is from the mid-1950s to the end of the 1960s. In the minds of many people, this period represented the halcyon days of LT, with a well presented bus and coach fleet. This was prior to the Country Area and Green Line coach operations being transferred to the newly-formed National Bus Company subsidiary, London Country Bus Services ("LCBS"), on 1 January 1970, and before the blight caused by a generation of unsuccessful vehicle types introduced in the late 1960s and early 1970s began to have a significant impact. The Underground did not suffer from new stock problems in the same way and modernising was no doubt welcomed by the travelling public although the archaic and varied stock still in service at the start of the 1960s (and in some cases even into the '70s) was missed by enthusiasts.

This album begins with a look at the vintage and slightly less elderly tube and surface stock in existence in the period under review, together with associated steam locomotives and some departmental road vehicles. We then move on to London's much loved trams, whose last day of service occurred on 5 July 1952. The onset of World War 2 had provided a reprieve for those trams mainly operating south of the River, with a further delay arising from a shortage of buses following the cessation of hostilities. Before the War, trolleybuses had replaced trams but the greater flexibility of motor buses evidenced through emergency re-routeings arising from enemy bombing convinced LT that post-war conversion of tram routes should be by buses. This did not, however, stop LT from ordering a fleet of new trolleybuses to replace its first examples (nicknamed "Diddlers"). Images of the post-war trolleybuses, together with pre-war and wartime examples, appear in the segment devoted to this type of electric vehicle. Declining passenger numbers caused the early withdrawal of some of the oldest trolleybuses in the mid-1950s but the programmed replacement of these vehicles by motor buses began in 1959. The final day of trolleybus operation in

London was Tuesday 8 May 1962. I remember it well because it was a school day and I managed to persuade my long-suffering mother to write a letter, much against her will, to my school in Ealing asking for me to be excused lessons that afternoon on the grounds of having an urgent dental appointment, thereby enabling me to go to Kingston and witness the ceremonial run. Brand new Routemasters were meant to replace the trolleybuses when the conversion to bus operation commenced but in the event the building programme fell behind schedule and RTs were used exclusively for the first three conversion stages.

The final segment of this album is devoted to buses and because of the dearth of hitherto unpublished colour images covering the pre-RT generation (sadly confined to just one picture of STLs) it is inevitably the RT type, including the Leyland variants, which dominates this portrayal. Taken together there were almost 7000 of these superb vehicles carrying passengers through the streets of central London, its suburbs and the surrounding countryside at various times between 1939 and 1979. The RT's contemporaries, the RF (including variants), GS, RLH and T classes are also covered.

The last bus type designed by LT to cope with the capital's demanding operational requirements – traffic congestion, overloading, short distances between bus stops, etc – was of course the famous Routemaster (RM). Despite its withdrawal from normal service in 2005 it is still possible to travel on a handful of these iconic vehicles on "heritage" sections of Routes 9 and 15 between Kensington High Street, Trafalgar Square and Tower Hill.

Whereas there are but a few original Routemasters operating in central London there will eventually be 600 new generation "Routemasters". I am referring of course to the new British-built bus specifically designed for London, the so-called "Borismaster", classified "LT". It is a huge diesel-hybrid vehicle with three entrances/exits, including an open platform, and two staircases. After a handful had been trialled on route 38, the first service to be converted to this type was route 24, from June 2013, but, being well outside the time line, you won't find any appearing in this album!

It is hoped that this book will rekindle happy memories of LT's operations some 40-plus years ago when many of us were travelling across or into London armed with our Ian Allan spotting books. Nostalgia is of course also fostered through the preservation movement and three fairly recent events are worthy of particular mention: (i) the repatriation of two more London trolleybuses making a total of nine located in Britain, a phenomenal eight of which were in operation for the 60th anniversary event at Carlton Colville; (ii) the transfer of the collection belonging to the London Bus Preservation Trust ("LBPT") from Cobham Bus Museum to the new London Bus Museum situated in the grounds of the historic Brooklands Museum; and (iii) the celebrations for the 150th anniversary of the Underground.

As regards the photographic material used in this book, the majority has been sourced from the Online Transport Archive, a registered charity holding a vast repository of cine films, colour slides and monochrome prints and negatives deposited there by enthusiasts or their surviving families for preservation/conservation and for the use and enjoyment of future generations. I am also grateful to the following individual contributors: Michael Wickham, Nick Lera, John May, John Bath, Michael Harries, Neil Davenport, Roy Hobbs, Rodney Lissenden, Blake Paterson, Robert Bridger (for use of Charles Firminger's photographs), John Carter (for use of his late father's photographs) and Richard Morant (for use of his late brother's photographs). Thanks are also due to Martin Jenkins, Piers Connor and Maurice Bateman for additional information and to Mike Eyre and Mike Russell for revitalising several damaged images.

In this book the abbreviation "LT" covers the London Passenger Transport Board and its successors starting from inception on 1 July 1933. Other abbreviations used are "Met", standing for the Metropolitan Railway and its successor, LT's Metropolitan Line, "BR" for British Railways and "GWR" for Great Western Railway.

Kevin R. McCormack
July 2013, Ashtead, Surrey

FACING PAGE TOP An eastbound Piccadilly Line train of Standard (pre-1938) stock and an engineering train hauled by the original L90 hurtle towards our fearless photographer (an LT Underground employee) near Barons Court. L90, previously ex-GWR pannier tank No 7711, was purchased by LT in October 1956 and was exchanged for one in better condition (No 7760) in September 1961 when it went to Swindon for intended overhaul. *Harry Luff/Online Transport Archive*

FACING PAGE BOTTOM In 1903, the Central London Railway ordered 64 new motor cars of forlorn appearance to replace its unsatisfactory electric locomotives. These cars lasted until 1939, at which point 36 were rebuilt into 18 electric sleet locomotives (ESLs) by joining two motor ends together. In August 1968, one such ESL stands at Neasden depot amongst a variety of stock including Bo-Bo locomotive No 1 *John Lyon*, surprisingly passed over for static preservation in favour of No 5. *Author*

ABOVE Five trailer cars built by Cammell Laird for the Piccadilly Line in 1920 and withdrawn from passenger service in 1938 were later converted into a mechanical engineering instruction unit. The train, seen here on display at the Underground Centenary Exhibition at Neasden depot on 25/26 May 1963, was scrapped in 1969. *Marcus Eavis/Online Transport Archive*

The flowers are blooming at Oakwood in May 1955 as a Piccadilly Line train formed of Standard stock proceeds to the northern terminus of Cockfosters, the next station. This design of stock was built between 1923 and 1934 with slight differences, operating for the last time on the Central Line on 22 June 1963. Forty-three carriages enjoyed an extended lifespan on the Isle of Wight by being converted to operate on BR's third rail system, the surviving Island line from Ryde to Shanklin having been electrified to replace steam traction. BR was unable to use normal electric trains because of limited clearances, hence the decision to purchase old tube stock. The standard stock was superseded by ex-LT 1938 stock around 1990 and five cars have since been repatriated for preservation. *Raymond DeGroote/Online Transport Archive*

LT took over services between Liverpool Street and Ongar from BR on 25 September 1949, creating an extension of the Central Line, but did not complete electrification of the final section from Epping to Ongar until 18 November 1957. During this eight-year period, LT hired a steam push and pull train from BR using Class F5 2-4-2 tanks to operate on the non-electrified section and this photograph depicts the interchange at Epping, featuring Standard tube stock and locomotive No 67200 from Stratford shed. Despite electrification, passenger numbers on the section beyond Epping declined to such an extent that LT closed the line on 30 September 1994. It has now re-opened as the Epping-Ongar Railway, a privately-owned heritage line.

Julian Thompson/Online Transport Archive

FACING PAGE TOP In 1935, four experimental 6-car trains, split into 2-car units, were introduced. These trains, three of which were initially semi-streamlined, provided improved traction performance as well as increased passenger accommodation due to the electrical equipment being located beneath the underframe. The fourth train was not streamlined and one of its motor cars heads a Central Line Epping service at Ongar in summer 1959, being distinguishable from subsequent 1938 stock by the square-shaped marker lights and the rounded top of the driver's door. *Marcus Eavis/Online Transport Archive*

FACING PAGE BOTTOM New 1938 stock, largely based on the 1935 experimental trains, but without streamlining, took over operation of the Northern Line, and eventually the Bakerloo

Line as well. With a converted Standard stock trailer added to the formation, a Bakerloo Line train waits at Headstone Lane on 6 June 1957. Bakerloo Line services to this station and onwards to Watford Junction were withdrawn on 24 October 1982. *Marcus Eavis/Online Transport Archive*

ABOVE 1938 stock trailer No 10306 was fitted in 1949 with additional windows to improve visibility for standing passengers. The extra glazing was unique to this carriage until the introduction of the 1967 Victoria Line stock (although this stock only had upper glazing fitted to the doors). No 10306, seen here at Finchley Central on the Northern Line, was also easily identifiable by its curious oval windows. It was scrapped in 1980. *John Bath collection*

Post-war production of new tube trains commenced in 1949 with motor cars and trailer cars of almost identical appearance to the 1938 stock. It was not until 1956 that a new design emerged in the form of three unpainted aluminium trains which were the forerunners of the 1959 stock intended as replacements for the elderly Standard stock on the Piccadilly Line. One such train of 1959 stock is depicted at Ruislip in summer 1961. The last running of 1959 stock in normal service occurred in January 2000 but an operational heritage set survives. *Marcus Eavis/Online Transport Archive*

In 1960 twelve prototype motor cars of a new design were constructed by Cravens to run with suitably adapted Standard stock. However, it was subsequently decided not to build further 1960 stock of this type and instead to produce more trains similar in design to the 1959 stock, known as 1962 stock. The 1960 stock was then modified in 1963 to trial automatic train operation (ATO) on the Central Line's Woodford-Hainault loop, as seen here on 18 May 1964 at Grange Hill. This was a precursor to ATO operation on the new Victoria Line by 1967 tube stock. *Marcus Eavis/Online Transport Archive*

Notable for being the only Underground trains to have been built in Scotland (by Hurst Nelson of Motherwell), the District Railway's C stock was delivered in 1911. Together with the subsequent D and E stock, they were withdrawn in the 1950s, ending their days on Kensington Olympia services until replaced by newer stock more appropriate for Exhibition visitors. However, on withdrawal some were converted into Stores Vans including this C stock motor car, SC 638, which is coupled to an E stock vehicle, this latter class having elliptical rather than clerestory roofs. SC 638's final passenger stock number had been 4214 and it became a Stores Van in July 1958, being withdrawn in March 1963. *Harry Luff/Online Transport Archive*

Instantly recognisable by its oval end windows and multiplicity of doors (the latter feature being particularly useful in the rush-hour), the District Railway's F stock was introduced in 1920. Displaced by R stock around 1950, the fleet was then transferred to the Metropolitan Line for use on semi-fast services. This photograph depicts F stock having passed Dollis Hill station in May 1955 travelling from Baker Street to Uxbridge. The last F stock working on the Uxbridge line was on 15 March 1963 and final passenger operation was on the East London line on 7 September 1963. *Raymond DeGroote/Online Transport Archive*

FACING PAGE The District Railway G class consisted of 50 motor cars with straight-ended clerestory roofs introduced in 923. Initially they worked with older stock and later with K, L, M and N classes (1927/31/35 stock) which differed from the G class by having rounded clerestory ends. Eventually, these rains were classified Q stock and included some flared-sided trailers, with the result that a Q stock train could contain three types of vehicle of varying appearance. The 1923-built motor cars were redesignated Q23 and one such vehicle, running with 927/31/35 stock, is pictured leaving Upminster Bridge station or Upminster in May 1955. A train with a flared-sided trailer s seen at High Street, Kensington. *Raymond DeGroote/Online Transport Archive; Harry Luff/Online Transport Archive*

ABOVE A London-bound Metropolitan Line train heads away from the camera at Rayners Lane in May 1955 composed of O/P stock built between 1936 and 1940. These units were sometimes known as Metadyne stock as a result of being fitted with this type of traction control equipment (which was later removed). The Holden-style station building designed by R H Uren dates from 1938 and replaced a more basic structure.
Raymond DeGroote/Online Transport Archive

FACING PAGE TOP Red O/P stock meets brown T stock at Moorgate on the Circle/Metropolitan Line. World War 2 bomb damage and the start of redevelopment in the area can be seen in this late 1950s view. *Harry Luff/Online Transport Archive*

FACING PAGE BOTTOM R stock was introduced in 1949 to replace remaining hand-worked door stock, some of the vehicles being new (designated R47 and R49) and others consisting of converted Q stock (designated R38). Further R stock was subsequently required, culminating in the R59 cars. As evidenced by this view on the District Line at Barking, the external design of the R stock was almost identical to the earlier O/P stock, apart from the absence of door push buttons and the fitting of an upper roller destination blind. *Author's collection*

ABOVE The electrification of the Met mainline as far as Harrow in 1905 rendered the Company's old rigid-wheelbase, flat-sided steam-hauled stock superfluous. Two batches of seven 8-wheeled coaches dating from 1884-7 were sold to France in 1909 and 1914 and operated in the Gironde district near Bordeaux but had fallen into disuse when photographed in 1960 at Lacanau. Fortunately, a shorter 4-wheeled coach of similar design (Jubilee stock carriage No 353 built in 1892) survives, owned by the LT Museum and rebuilt for the Underground 150 celebrations in 2013. *Harry Luff/Online Transport Archive*

FACING PAGE The next generation of steam carriages, the Bogie stock, was also affected by the 1905 electrification extension and was converted to electric working between 1906 and 1924. Following withdrawal of this stock, six carriages were converted back to steam operation in 1940 to form two 3-coach push-and-pull sets (one set in use at a time) for the Chesham branch. These views taken shortly before electrification of the branch in September 1960 depict LT carriage No 518 (Met No 394), built by Ashbury in 1900 and now operating on the Bluebell Railway, waiting to be propelled out of Chalfont & Latimer station and then the train leaving the station for Chesham behind Ivatt 2-6-2 tank No 41284. *Marcus Eavis/Online Transport Archive*

ABOVE In May 1955, Bo-Bo electric locomotive No 11 *George Romney*, still carrying grey livery, approaches Rickmansworth station with one of the Chesham sets of Bogie stock, presumably to effect an exchange with the second set. Another electric locomotive, by now restored to maroon livery, stands at the head of a train of Dreadnought stock, the first compartment of which is designated "Ladies Only". These carriages were the standard locomotive-hauled compartment stock built between 1910 and 1923, albeit the earliest were rebuilds of 1905 stock, one of which, No 427, survives along with two later coaches, Nos 465 and 509, on the Keighley & Worth Valley Railway. *Raymond DeGroote/Online Transport Archive*

No 6 *William Penn* stands at Rickmansworth in May 1955. Twenty of these powerful locomotives were built between 1921 and 1923, replacing twenty smaller locomotives dating from 1904-6. The first locomotive, No 17, was a rebuild of the original machine but this was considered unsatisfactory (indeed, No 17 was the first to be withdrawn, in 1943) and the remainder were virtually new constructions. The grey livery was introduced from 1943 due to wartime paint scarcity and to facilitate cleaning, the ornate bronze name-plates also being removed. *Raymond DeGroote/Online Transport Archive*

Two T-class electric units stand at Watford (Met) in May 1955. This compartment stock was built between 1927 and 1931, the last batch being externally steel-panelled (as evidenced by the Wembley Park train) whereas the earlier examples (as depicted on the right) had teak bodies, distinguishable by their mouldings. The last LT running of T stock was in October 1962 but two steel motor coaches, Nos 2758 and 2749, which had been converted into electric sleet locomotives (ESL 118A and 118B respectively) survive and are currently on the Spa Valley Railway. *Raymond DeGroote/Online Transport Archive*

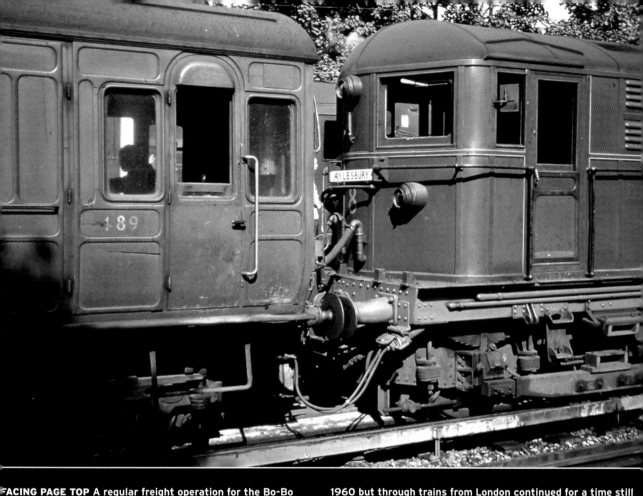

FACING PAGE TOP A regular freight operation for the Bo-Bo electrics was to take coal to Chiltern Court flats in London, the last journey being made on 3 August 1961 hauled by No 7. The earlier working shown here at Baker Street has No 2 *Thomas Lord* in charge, this locomotive's former identity of *Oliver Cromwell* not being restored when new name plates were cast and maroon livery re-introduced from October 1953. *Harry Luff/Online Transport Archive*

FACING PAGE BOTTOM Old meets new at Chesham in summer 1961. The replacement for F stock, T stock and locomotive hauled trains came in the form of A60 and A62 Cravens cars. The steam shuttle service was electrified from 12 September

1960 but through trains from London continued for a time still using Bo-Bo electric locomotives hauling "Dreadnought" carriages In this view No 16 *Oliver Goldsmith* passes A60 stock standing in the new bay platform. *Marcus Eavis/Online Transport Archive*

ABOVE In this image from summer 1961, Bo-Bo electric locomotive No 8 *Sherlock Holmes* has just coupled up to an Aylesbury-London Metropolitan Line train at Rickmansworth following removal of the steam locomotive just visible in the background. The "Dreadnought" coach, No 489, is showing signs of age with patches and splits in the woodwork and with a steel plate fitted to the lower section of the door. *Marcus Eavis/Online Transport Archive*

RIGHT Met No 23 (later L45), built in 1866, is the sole survivor of 120 Beyer-Peacock 4-4-0 tank engines divided between the Met and the District which were the mainstay of passenger services on both railways until electrification commenced in the early 1900s. All but five of the Beyer Peacock engines were either sold or scrapped before LT took over on 1 July 1933 and No 23 was the only one to survive beyond World War 2, being withdrawn in 1948 and preserved by LT. This view depicts the locomotive on display in its 1903 condition at the Underground Centenary Exhibition at Neasden on 25 May 1963. *Author*

Bus meets Underground at Hounslow West station, gateway to Heathrow Central in conjunction with the 81B bus service. This station was the terminus of the Hounslow branch of the Piccadilly Line (and, up to 1964, also the District Line) until the extension to Hatton Cross was opened in 1975 (later reaching Heathrow Airport). The station, originally called Hounslow Barracks, opened in 1884 and took its present name in 1925. The current surface building dates from 1931. The bus, T751, is working a 222 service from Uxbridge station to Hounslow Central station via London Airport (North). This route was converted to RF operation on 26 November 1958 and withdrawn on 15 March 1961. *Julian Thompson/Online Transport Archive*

On 5 July 1952, the last day that trams operated in London, the driver of this ex-West Ham car has just changed the points on one side of the Yorkshire Grey roundabout at the junction of Well Hall Road and Westhorne Avenue, Eltham. The conductor is leaning out ready to monitor the progress of the trolley through the junction. The overhead skates which normally controlled the workings of the points can be seen above and behind the car. Owing to the narrowness of the advertising panel on the ex-West Ham trams, these were unable to display the "Last Tram Week" posters. Taken over by LT in 1933, a number of the ex-West Ham bogie cars, ̲̲̲̲̲̲̲̲̲̲̲ from 1925 to 1931, were in service on the final day. *E. E. A. Ward/Online T̲̲̲̲̲̲t Archive*

At the head of a trio of trams waiting for an ex-West Ham car to clear the crossover at Eltham Green on 5 July 1952 is one of the 100 E/3 class cars delivered to the London County Council ("LCC") in 1931 for use in the remodelled Kingsway Subway (closed April 1952). Built by Hurst Nelson, the E/3s had flush-sided, all-metal bodies and rode on EMB maximum traction bogies. Immediately behind is an ex-East Ham car. All three trams in the line-up have the "Last Tram Week" notice and their double trolleys can clearly be seen. These obviated the need for the conductor to swing the trolley in the middle of busy roads. This view was taken on one of the outer sections where power was drawn from the overhead wires and some of the last tramway extensions in London were in this area. *F. E. J. Ward/Online Transport Archive*

Another last day view of an ex-LCC E/3 in Woolwich Road, Charlton, this time on one of the conduit sections. The final tram to bus change-over, which took place during the night of 5/6 July 1952, involved six routes and two depots. It also marked the end of conduit operation in Britain. This mode of electric traction, whereby power was obtained through a slot in the road, was determined by a need to avoid visually obtrusive wires and poles in sensitive parts of the capital. In this view, car No 1926 heads away from the camera, having just passed the appropriately named Felltram Way leading to Charlton Works, where trams were rebuilt, repaired and overhauled. Round the corner from the now demolished Woolwich Road school (the bell tower of which is visible) and a small distance beyond was Penhall Road scrapyard. This had been specially built and between 1950 and early 1953 disposed of hundreds of redundant trams. Within a few hours, No 1926 would make its final journey to this "burning ground".

F. E. J. Ward/Online Transport Archive

LT's most modern trams were the "Felthams", so named because they were built by the Union Construction & Finance Company (UCC) at Feltham, Middlesex, a company that was part of the Underground group. Dating from 1931, these trams were inherited from London United Tramways and Metropolitan Electric Tramways in 1933 and then, as a result of the tram to trolleybus conversion programme north of the River, all 100 production cars were transferred south of the River to Telford Avenue depot near Streatham Hill, mostly in 1936. In this view, No 2088 is seen outside the depot during a crew change in 1949. Later, most of the "Felthams" saw further service in Leeds, with the last survivors being withdrawn in 1959. The Pullman Court apartment block seen in the background was built in 1936 and now has listed building status, being an excellent example of Modernist architecture.

Jack Law/Online Transport Archive

Pursued by a film cameraman and stared at by onlookers, Class A1 trolleybus No 1, which was delivered to London United Tramways ("LUT") in January 1931, passes over Kingston Bridge on its ceremonial run to mark the end of trolleybus operation in London on 8 May 1962. The vehicles belonging to Classes A1 and A2 were nicknamed "Diddlers" and the bodies, on AEC chassis, were constructed ... after the "Feltham" trams. The "Diddlers" lasted until 1948 when they were

After inheriting the 60-strong A1 and A2 classes LT began expanding the trolleybus fleet, with the new British built vehicles being of similar basic appearance despite detail differences and looking nothing like the "Diddlers". However, a shortage of trolleybuses during World War 2 resulted in LT being allowed to acquire 43 strange-looking Leylands and AECs intended for Durban and Johannesburg, which were unlikely ever to have reached South Africa due to enemy submarine activity. As well as containing several features untypical of LT vehicles, these trolleybuses exceeded width and weight regulations but dispensation was given by the authorities for these to operate, albeit they were confined to the Ilford area. One of the intended Johannesburg exports, SA3 class No 1753, is seen at Barkingside, this view clearly showing the panelled over front exit door not required for London.
Ron Copson/Online Transport Archive

ABOVE Trolleybus No 770 belonged to the H1 class of Metro-Cammell-bodied Leylands introduced in 1938. The vehicle is working from Wood Green depot and is making its way from Enfield to Tottenham Court Road on a 629 service. This route was a victim of Stage 10 of the trolleybus replacement programme, final running being on 25 April 1961.
Julian Thompson/Online Transport Archive

FACING PAGE TOP A trolleybus route with a suffix to its number was Stamford Hill depot's Sundays-only 649A from Wood Green LT station to Liverpool Street station which ran from 17 April 1949 until its demise on 16 July 1961. Seen here in High Road, Tottenham, this service is worked by all-Leyland Class K1 vehicle, No 1148. The ornate building to the right is the Grade II Listed Tottenham Palace which opened in 1908 as a Music Hall and Variety Theatre. *Marcus Eavis/Online Transport Archive*

FACING PAGE BOTTOM Class Q1 No 1856 hurries through Uxbridge town centre in May 1955 with a 607 service to Shepherds Bush. On the left is one of the pre-war F1 class which had been the mainstay of this route operated from Hanwell depot. The 607, which had replaced tram route 7 from 15 November 1936, was itself superseded by RM-operated bus route 207 (with some RTs from Uxbridge garage used on Sundays) following its withdrawal on 8 November 1960 upon implementation of conversion Stage 8.
Raymond DeGroote/Online Transport Archive

Until buses took over, Stratford Broadway was a busy trolleybus hub with routes 669, 689 and 690 terminating there and routes 661, 663 and 695 passing through. On a very hot and sultry 1959 day (judging by the open windows), Class L3 No 1382 and Class N1 No 1637 stand in the foreground, the latter being about to make its way to Aldgate. Route 661 was a Stage 3 conversion with trolleybuses running for the final time on 18 August 1959. Route 690 lasted until 2 February 1960 when Stage 5 was implemented.

Marcus Eavis/Online Transport Archive

Another Stage 3 conversion victim was route 693 and in this 1959 scene at Ilford Broadway, No 1744 of Class SA2 and No 1760 of Class SA3 (both originally destined for Durban and Johannesburg respectively) are depicted. With their extra width (8ft-wide bodies on 7ft 6in-wide chassis), they were at the time LT's widest vehicles but lost this unique status soon after the end of the war when the Q1 trolleybuses and RTW motor buses were introduced. Sadly, all 43 of these unique LT trolleybuses were broken up but a British-built example exported to Johannesburg which strongly resembles the SA3 vehicles has been repatriated and is preserved at the Trolleybus Museum at Sandtoft. *Marcus Eavis/Online Transport Archive*

ABOVE Arguably, the most handsome London trolleybuses were those members of the C2 and C3 classes (99 out of 200 vehicles), together with the unique D1, which were fitted with rear wheel spats. Class C3 No 289, built in 1936, was one of those so adorned and is seen working a 662 service which operated between Sudbury (Swan) and Paddington Green. Although the 662 ran until 2 January 1962 when the penultimate conversion stage (13) came into effect, the last C2s and C3s were withdrawn in November 1959 and replaced by redundant newer trolleybuses. *Julian Thompson/Online Transport Archive*

FACING PAGE Facing Custom House railway station, Class L3 No 1400 is about to turn from Freemasons Road into Victoria Docks Road on 23 April 1960, three days before implementation of Stage 6 of the trolleybus replacement programme. The vehicle is heading for the southern terminus at Victoria & Albert Docks but the blinds have already been changed to the northern terminus, Crooked Billet, a destination which must have puzzled anyone unaware that this was a watering hole in Walthamstow. At the same location but heading in the reverse direction to Chingford Mount is Class M1 trolleybus No 1530. The backdrop to both these pictures has changed beyond all recognition, the Railway Tavern having been replaced by the Customs House Hotel at 272-283 Victoria Docks Road. *Both: Charles Firminger*

The end of trolleybus operation in London occurred on 8 May 1962 when Fulwell and Isleworth depots' routes were withdrawn on implementation of Stage 14 of the conversion programme. This view of the interior of Fulwell depot was taken a few weeks before the demise of the trolleybuses and shows early wartime L3 class vehicles which were drafted in to those depots following the sale of the post-war Q1s to Spain. Fulwell depot was built in 1902 for the new electric trams, with trolleybuses arriving in 1931 and the

Fast forward to 11 October 1969 and a solitary trolleybus, LT Museum's Class K2 No 1253, is receiving attention in the unlikely company of Routemasters and Merlins at Fulwell. Amazingly, there are believed to be as many as 13 London trolleybuses surviving. In Britain these are Nos 1, 260, 796 (repatriated from France), 1201, 1253, 1348 (repatriated from Ireland), 1521, 1768 and 1812 (repatriated from Spain), all being either at the East Anglia Transport Museum at Carlton Colville, the Trolleybus Museum at Sandtoft or the LT Museum. Another four exist in Spain: Nos 1836, 1837, 1838 and 1839, three of which have been preserved in local liveries. *Online Transport Archive*

Route 654 was one of three routes to be withdrawn under Stage 1 of the trolleybus to motor bus conversion scheme, ceasing to operate after 3 March 1959, by which time the service was worked by the oldest trolleybuses in the fleet, the 30-strong B1 class dating from 1935. Because of the undulating nature of the route, in particular Anerley Hill, the B1s were short vehicles (with 60 seats instead of the normal 70 seats) and fitted with special braking equipment. The entire class was based at Carshalton depot (in Westmead Road, Sutton) for route 654 (Sutton Green-Crystal Palace) and in this summer 1958 view No 86 rests at the Crystal Palace terminus. *Julian Thompson/Online Transport Archive*

ABOVE AND RIGHT The trolleybus routes around Kingston might have survived for several years beyond 1962 had the Spanish not made an offer to purchase the post-war Q1 vehicles. This resulted in the unexpected withdrawal of the type and their replacement by redundant older vehicles pending the imposition of an additional and final conversion stage on 8 May 1962. The change in 1961 of vehicle types on Fulwell depot's route 604 (Hampton Court–Wimbledon) is illustrated here by Q1 No 1787 standing at the Hampton Court terminus and Class L3 No 1445 approaching Kingston. *Ron Copson/Online Transport Archive; Author*

Class L3 trolleybus No 1502 approaches Hampton Wick on its journey from Teddington to Wimbledon. For some reason everyone seems to have piled onto the lower deck! The 150-strong L3 class were chassisless AEC vehicles with Metro-Cammell bodies. They began to enter service in summer 1939 and most remained in operation until the cessation of trolleybus operation on 8 May 1962, obtaining a short stay of execution as a result of the sale of the post-war Q1 class to Spain. *Neil Davenport*

RIGHT AND BELOW RIGHT
Pursued by a roofbox RT, Class L3 trolleybus No 1518 is working a 667 service towards Brentford on 27 April 1961, having just passed under the Chiswick Flyover. This structure was subsequently incorporated into the M4 as portrayed in this view looking westwards towards Brentford in summer 1964. The approaching vehicle is a British European Airways ("BEA") AEC Regal IV, MLL 739, carrying airline passengers from Heathrow to the West London Air Terminal at Gloucester Road. There were 65 of these 8ft wide coaches, with chassis similar to the RFW coaches. The LT-designed Park Royal bodywork seated 37 passengers.
Both: Nick Lera

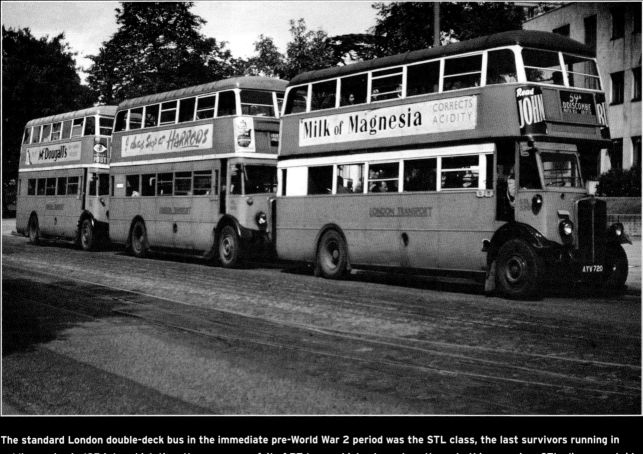

The standard London double-deck bus in the immediate pre-World War 2 period was the STL class, the last survivors running in public service in 1954, by which time there was a surfeit of RT type vehicles to replace them. In this rare view, STLs line up outside Telford Avenue tram depot, Streatham Hill, in 1949, headed by STL 570 dating from 1934. This bus was withdrawn from passenger service in March 1953 and then became a trainer until final withdrawal in March 1955. Two similar "leaning-back" STLs have survived: STL 441 preserved by the LBPT and STL 469 in the LT Museum Collection. Other complete class members to survive are STLs 2093 and 2377, also belonging to the LBPT, and post-war STL 2692. In addition, front-entrance country STL 1470 is preserved in its final tree-lopper condition. *Jack Law/Online Transport Archive*

LT's Green Line coach services were withdrawn for most of World War 2 and luxury Green Line coach T 504, which had entered service in 1938, was converted into an ambulance towards the end of 1939. Returned to Green Line service in 1946, it ended its operational life with LT as a red bus at Kingston in 1954, whereupon it was sold. Subsequent plans to convert it firstly into a mobile showroom and then into a mobile crane never materialised and the bus remained intact in a scrapyard at Chadderton, near Oldham, until spotted by enthusiasts travelling on a passing train and rescued in 1968. In this view, T 504 is still carrying its LT blinds for the Kingston area, with "Upper Halliford" just visible. It has now been restored to Green Line coach condition by the LBPT. A sister vehicle, T 499, has been repatriated from Australia by Ensignbus. *John Bath collection*

Several STLs were exported when withdrawn by LT including STL 1583 which saw further service in Spain. Fitted with bodywork constructed by LT at Chiswick Works, this vehicle had entered service at Cricklewood garage in September 1936 and ended its LT passenger duties at Barking in May 1953. After serving for a while as a trainer this bus was sold to a dealer in April 1954. On 19 September 1961 it was spotted in Valencia, with its staircase reversed and additional opening windows fitted. Carrying a Madrid registration plate (M-130.972), the STL is wearing the livery of Empresas F. Lerma of Buñol, now known as Autobuses Buñol.

Charles Firminger

The first of nearly 7000 members of the RT family entered service in August 1939 and a further 150 were constructed through to January 1942, by which time wartime restrictions had brought the building programme to a halt. RT construction recommenced in 1947 and by 1955 it was possible to withdraw from passenger duties the wartime RTs (colloquially but inaccurately called "pre-war RTs"), which were by then LT's oldest operational buses. However, seven were retained, painted green and dispatched to Hertford garage for route 327 to replace post-war STLs (yes, older buses replacing newer buses) because the latter were non-standard and buyers had been found for them. Route 327 operated over a weak bridge at Broxbourne and post-war RTs exceeded the weight limit, whereas the "pre-war" RTs, like the post-war STLs, were lighter. The selected seven worked from May 1955 to August 1957, by which time the offending bridge had been rebuilt. Here we see RT 128 in Hertford, heading for Nazeing.

Julian Thompson/Online Transport Archive

LEFT With only two months of passenger service remaining, Brixton garage's RTW 5 climbs the hump bridge in White Horse Road over the railway line between Thornton Heath and Selhurst stations on 13 March 1966. Brixton was the last operator of RTWs (all-Leyland 8ft-wide RTs), their last day being 14 May 1966, and this particular vehicle was purchased by the Ceylon Transport Board at the end of the year. RTWs had replaced RTLs on Sunday route 57A in April 1964 and were in turn replaced by RMs in May 1966. *Rodney Lissenden*

ABOVE Three variations of RTL stand outside Victoria station in October 1965. On the extreme left is one of the Metro-Cammell-bodied vehicles, RTL 653, identifiable by its narrower central relief band. In the centre is RTL 409 carrying an old RT 10 roofbox body (in anticipation of the vehicle's early withdrawal) which it received in 1964. On the right is RTL 1620, a more conventional RTL and one which was stored for four years following completion, only entering service in March 1958. In effect, LT had over-ordered RT family vehicles in expectation of additional services being introduced and not anticipating the downturn in passenger numbers arising from increased car ownership. *Michael Wickham collection*

On the edge of Hampstead Heath, crew-operated RF 393 negotiates the Spaniards Road bend, between the historic Spaniards Inn on the left and the toll house on the right, on 1 July 1967. Being a particularly hilly route, the 210 was selected to be the first RF-operated service in the Central Area, replacement of the Qs and TDs then in use commencing on 11 September 1952. The route was converted to one-person operation on 24 January 1970, still using RFs, these operating until 17 September 1971 when unreliable AEC Swifts took over. The inn is reputed to have been a favourite watering hole of the famous highwayman, Dick Turpin. The toll gate marked the entrance to the Bishop of London's estate and still constitutes a boundary, with the Inn being located in the London Borough of Barnet and the toll house in the London Borough of Camden. *Michael Wickham collection*

Much travelled RT 2776, seen here in Ferndale Street on a visit to Cyprus (the one in Newham!) in June 1965, toured America and Canada in March – August 1952, covering some 12,000 miles. Three LT buses made the trip in furtherance of a "Come to Britain" tourist campaign, the other two being RT 2775 (preserved by the LBPT) and RTL 1307. RT 2776 was the "rides" bus and was fitted with additional ventilators, the two conspicuous ones in the roof plus one under the canopy, for increased passenger comfort in warmer climes. Buses carrying GB plates for overseas travel were meant to have their chassis and bodies kept together on overhaul

An amended order by Midland General for Weymann-built low height bodies on Regent III chassis (30 ordered but only 10 required) resulted in LT buying the surplus vehicles (numbering them RLH 1-20) and then ordering a further 56, thereby enabling it to update the entire lowbridge fleet. There were only four Central Area lowbridge double decker routes, the majority of such routes being in the Country Area. RLH 17 entered service in July 1950 and was transferred from the Country Area to the Central Area, without being repainted, in December 1964, remaining at Harrow Weald garage for route 230 until its withdrawal in November 1966. Here it is on 7 May 1966 in Christchurch Avenue, Kenton. Many RLHs were exported at the end of their lives with LT, but not RLH 17 which was sold to a biscuit company for use as staff transport and broken up in 1971. *Michael Wickham collection.*

RIGHT In May 1969 Leatherhead garage's RT 3116 blends in well with the leafy surroundings of Burford Bridge, at the foot of Box Hill, as it makes its marathon journey from Dorking to Chelsham via Epsom, Sutton and Croydon. It's a far cry from today's 470 service which is operated by Epsom Coaches with red Optare single-deckers although the current journey from Epsom to Colliers Wood does cover part of the old route. *Michael Harries/Author's collection*

BELOW RIGHT Lost in Ealing! Two RMs find themselves off-route in early 1964, at a time when the RT-operated 97 service was endowed with some RMs on Sundays. On this occasion a burst water main in Eaton Rise necessitated an unplanned diversion. RM 418 has climbed Castlebar Road (not then served by buses), and just turned into Montpelier Avenue (on the 65 bus route) in order to reach Woodfield Road while the second RM heads for Ealing Broadway. Of course, in the dark this scene could be anywhere – only the photographer (then at school in Montpelier Avenue and living nearby) knows the exact location! *Author*

ABOVE Uxbridge bus station, where these three views were taken, was one of the locations where Central Area buses intermingled with their Country Area cousins, as illustrated here by RT 3232 and RT 1812 plus others of this type, as well as RF 601 and three RMLs. RT 3232 was transferred to London Country on 1 January 1970, reacquired by LT in September 1972 and repainted red, withdrawn in November 1979, and then purchased by Ensignbus for preservation. This view dates from June 1968. *Michael Wickham collection*

FACING PAGE TOP Stepping back to the 1950s, the post-war, archaic-looking T and TD classes, delivered between 1946 and 1948, were purchased as a stop-gap measure to enable the replacement of many of the ageing pre-war single-deckers prior to the introduction of the RF class. These examples, T 750 and T 762, were from a batch of 50 Weymann-bodied AEC Regals used in the Central Area. Uxbridge was the last garage to operate these "frowning" Ts, withdrawal coming in November 1958, with replacement by RFs and TDs, and the entire series was sold to Ceylon. *Geoff Morant*

FACING PAGE BOTTOM By early 1974, the old order was confined to RFs (Nos 350 and 418 visible), with Swift single deckers and DMS-type double deckers dominating. *Marcus Eavis/Online Transport Archive*

There were 1631 Leyland-built RTLs, and the majority of the class received interchangeable Park Royal or Weymann bodies, but RTLs 551-1000 had Metro-Cammell bodies which were not interchangeable with the other types. These 450 buses were distinguishable by their narrower central relief band with thick upper moulding, as illustrated in this view of RTL 915 standing outside Minster House, 272-274 Vauxhall Bridge Road, on a rush-hour working of route 185 to the Blackwall Tunnel. Metro-Cammell had originally been contracted to build 1000 RTL bodies which had been the intended total of narrow double-deck Leylands, but due to various complications, the Birmingham company ended up building just 450 but received a bonus in the form of a contract to build all 700 RF bodies. *John Bath collection*

The 84-strong Guy Special class with Eastern Coach Works bodies originated in 1953 and was designed to replace the Leyland Cubs operating on country routes with limited patronage and which used narrow lanes. At this time, single manning was only permitted on buses with a passenger capacity of up to 20 seats but the authorities allowed this to be extended to the 26-seater Guy Specials. GS 55, one of many now preserved, was based at Hertford when seen at Welwyn in December 1967. The need for these buses had declined in the 1960s with the abolition of uneconomic routes and the conversion of RFs to one-person operation following relaxation of the seating restriction. The last survivors ended their passenger service on 29 March 1972, under London Country auspices.
Michael Wickham collection

ABOVE The deserted shopping parade at Northwood in June 1968 is a reminder of Sundays when trading restrictions were still in force and car ownership was far from universal. The 336B was a Sundays-only service between Little Missenden and Northwood station worked on this occasion by Amersham-based Country RF 553. These vehicles received body exchanges during the Aldenham overhaul process and RF 553 has acquired a Green Line coach body, as evidenced by the roof board mounting brackets. The bus was in service for 20 years, being sold for scrap in 1973. *Michael Wickham collection*

FACING PAGE TOP Over half of the 500-strong RTW class were acquired by the Ceylon Transport Board, including this one, RTW 484, seen here on a route 39 working. RTWs were used on this north-south service (Camden-Southfields, with alterations) from 1951 to 1965. *Julian Thompson/Online Transport Archive*

FACING PAGE BOTTOM It would be hard to find another large operator's fleet of buses in such superb external condition as these LT vehicles laying over at New Barnet in July 1969. Viewed from left to right are RML 2419, RT 360, demoted Green Line coach RMC 1506 and RF 616. The RML is believed to be the only member of this line-up to survive today. *Michael Wickham collection*

LEFT AND BELOW LEFT
RM 1000, the Routemaster with the strange registration mark, was in its first month of service when photographed in March 1962 at North Woolwich in "as-built" condition (apart from replacement of its ceremonial "AEC/LT 1000th Routemaster" advertisements applied for its launch in October 1961). Withdrawn in 1985, this bus is now preserved. On the other hand, completion of the 1000th RT, which initially carried a Weymann roofbox body, does not appear to have been subject to any special ceremony, the bus simply entering service at Windsor garage in October 1948. RT 1000 was subsequently fitted with a later body and was working from Dunton Green garage when it was photographed in summer 1969 entering High Street, Sevenoaks, from Dartford Road. *Michael Wickham collection; Dave Brown/Author's collection*

RTW 398 is pursued by RTL 1221 in Baker Street, at the junction with Marylebone Road, on 29 April 1965. By this time new RMs, having ousted the trolleybuses, had started to replace the RTW fleet, resulting in many of the latter, being the same width (8ft) as RMs, becoming training buses. RTW 398 became a trainer in 1963 and was sold for scrap in 1969.

R. L. Wilson/Online Transport Archive

ABOVE RM 1740, seen here at Hammersmith in June 1973, had an interesting life. Entering service in November 1963, it carried all-over advertising for Danone between March and September 1973, became a skid bus at Chiswick Works in 1984 and was last heard of in Uruguay, where it was sent in 1991.
Harry Luff/Online Transport Archive

FACING PAGE TOP RTs rule in this early 1960s shot taken at Slough railway station. Accelerating into the picture is a Central Area RT on route 81 heading for Hounslow, passing Country Area RTs operating local services, led by RT 3118. The 446 group of routes was converted to one-person operation in March 1969 when Merlins took over. *John May*

FACING PAGE BOTTOM In the company of an RT on route 457A to Uxbridge, GS 77 lays over at the Windsor bus stand next to Burford House in St Alban's Street. The GS is working route 445 to Datchet Common, a service on which it was used from its entry into service in July 1954 through to withdrawal in October 1962. Following sale out of service, the bus was scrapped in 1968. *John May*

A Central Area directive was issued on 30 August 1963 stating that offside route numbers were no longer to be shown, resulting in RTs' holders being repainted from black to red or in some cases being removed and panelled over. The purpose of the edict was to deter potential passengers on the opposite side of the road from crossing in front of oncoming traffic. Peckham garage's RT 1564 displays the original fitting as it lays over in Shoreditch on 18 June 1960 while operating on route 78. Interestingly, a start has been made to attach flashing indicator "ears" above the central relief band near the front of the bus, a fitment pioneered on the Routemaster prototypes and extended across LT's fleet from 1959. *R. L. Wilson/Online Transport Archive*

Photographed at Chessington Zoo (now Chessington World of Adventures), RFW 6 (one of 15 Eastern Coach Works-bodied 8ft-wide Regal IVs) entered service with LT's Private Hire fleet in April 1951. The RFWs, together with the first twenty-five RFs, were introduced to modernise the fleet in time to cope with the anticipated large numbers of visitors to London for the Festival of Britain in summer 1951. The private hire coaches were noted for the glazed roof panels to facilitate sightseeing and were painted in a distinctive flake grey and Lincoln green livery with red lining and red-edged lettering. RFW 6 worked summer seasons up to 1964, after which it was withdrawn following the outsourcing of the private hire operation. Ten of the class were sold to Ceylon (Sri Lanka) and two of the remainder have been preserved including this example, now owned by the LBPT.

Harry Luff/Online Transport Archive

Heathrow Airport is host to two unique Routemasters in these views dating from August/September 1964.

LEFT The roof garden balconies of the Queen's Building are crowded with visitors who have arrived on the various coaches lined up on the right (including Green Line RF 43 from Crawley). Waiting at the bus terminus is the unpainted "Silver Lady", RM 664, which was spending a three-month stint at Fulwell garage during its tour of various garages between its entry into service in July 1961 and its being painted red in August 1965. The body was later transferred to RM 577 which is now preserved.

LEFT AND ABOVE The forward-entrance long Routemaster, RMF 1254 (also now preserved), which was later sold to Northern General, is seen here on loan to BEA for two years to trial the towing of luggage trailers as potential replacements for the airline's fleet of one-and-a-half-deck coaches, several of which feature here. However, the RM was considered too long for hauling a trailer and so the production version for BEA was built to the standard length. *All: Mike Harries/Author's collection*

FACING PAGE On their introduction in November 1965, the RC class of 14 Reliances with 49-seater Willowbrook coach bodies was heralded as representing Green Line's new modern image, hence the decision to paint them silver grey with a dark green waistband. Eye-catching they may have been but they were mechanically poor and were in and out of operation for up to twelve years until being withdrawn from public service in 1977 (except RC 11 which had been withdrawn in 1971 after catching fire). These views of RC 9 outside Windsor garage were taken on 28 November 1965. *Marcus Eavis/Online Transport Archive*

ABOVE In a further effort to update the appearance of the Green Line fleet following the poor performance of the RC class, LT instigated an RF cosmetic modernisation programme in 1966/7 involving 175 RFs, pending the arrival of successful new coaches. Those modernised included RF 156, photographed in Dorking during August 1968 at the start of its marathon journey to Luton via Victoria on route 714. The vehicle was withdrawn in January 1975 and sold for scrap.
Michael Harries/Author's collection

RIGHT Carrying an old RT3 roofbox body, Merton-based RT 767 travels under the trolleybus wires through Tooting in 1960 on tram replacement route 155, heading for Embankment. This bus entered service in August 1948 and was sold to Ceylon (Sri Lanka) in December 1964.
Michael Wickham collection

ABOVE and **LEFT** Seen here at Victoria station while working Red Arrow service 507, AEC Merlin MBA 588 sported an experimental red and white livery from September 1972 to March 1976. Donated to Feltham Community Association for use as a shop in October 1981, this vehicle was acquired for preservation in 2002 and is now at Wythall Transport Museum. Whereas MBA 588's colour scheme was vetoed, white relief around the upper deck window surrounds as seen on DMS 46 in High Street, Croydon, was experimentally carried by this vehicle from September 1974 and was then adopted for some classes for a few years. DMS 46 had entered service in January 1971 in all-red livery and it had reverted to this colour scheme when withdrawn in October 1981 and subsequently scrapped. *Both: Chris Evans*

LEFT The third member of the 500-strong RTW class, Chalk Farm's RTW 3, stands at the terminus of route 31 in Bayham Street, Camden. Route 31 was converted from RTL to RTW operation on 2 May 1951 and re-converted to RTLs on 1 November 1965, just after this picture was taken. RTW 3 was withdrawn in January 1966 and sold to Ceylon a year later.
Author's collection

RIGHT The coach service from Guildford to Hertford, illustrated here by RF 54 at Hertford, originated in 1929 under the auspices of Skylark Motor Services. This company was taken over by Green Line Coaches Ltd in 1932 which in turn was absorbed into London Transport in the following year. RFs were introduced on this service, now numbered 715, from December 1951 but were replaced by Routemaster coaches in August 1962 amidst a blaze of publicity. These lasted on the 715 until one-person operation was introduced in 1972.
Julian Thompson/Online Transport Archive

ABOVE RTL 384, fitted with an old roofbox body from an RT, looks in remarkably good condition for a vehicle facing impending withdrawal as it fills up with passengers at Aldgate bus station in summer 1966 while on a short working of route 40A. This service from Herne Hill to North Woolwich, normally worked by RMs, was introduced on 27 January 1965. *Author's collection*

LEFT AND BELOW LEFT
Operated from Dalston garage, LT's last lowbridge double-deck route, which heralded the demise of the RLH class, was the 178, introduced in May 1959 to replace the RF-worked 208A. To start operations, Merton garage's surplus red RLHs from the withdrawn 127 service were transferred. However, three additional RLHs were also required; these came from the Country Area and included RLH 29, seen here on 31 August 1968 in Waddington Street, Stratford. On 16 April 1971 RLHs and route 178 operated for the last time, whereupon various routes in the area were re-organised. This saw the arrival of AEC Swifts but in 1973 Dalston garage received six Metro-Scanias (MS 1-6) and six Leyland Nationals (LS 1-6) for comparison trials to determine which type should be selected as the new standard single-decker (the Nationals won). Brand new MS 6 turns out of Lower Clapton Road to reach the bus stand beside Clapton Pond. *Marcus Eavis/Online Transport Archive*; *Harry Luff/ Online Transport Archive*

ABOVE MBA 585 spent its entire working life from September 1969 to June 1981 allocated to Walworth (WL) garage for Red Arrow services. However, on 8 September 1974 it escaped from the metropolis to Epsom in the company of another, possibly to operate a race day shuttle service between the railway station and Epsom Downs. The platforms have obviously been raided to provide barrier supports! *Neil Davenport*

RIGHT "Dolly mixtures" (mainly Green Line ones) await the call of duty at Epsom station on Derby Day, 6 June 1973. *Neil Davenport*

ABOVE The unique front-entrance, rear-engined Routemaster, FRM 1, was delivered to LT in July 1966 and following extensive trials entered service at Tottenham garage in June 1967. After the bus caught fire on 31 August 1967, various modifications were made, including the fitting of some opening windows, and it returned to Tottenham where it remained until August 1969, after which it was adapted for one-person operation and sent to Croydon. This view shows the vehicle at Waterloo in summer 1968. *Harry Luff/Online Transport Archive*

FACING PAGE A vehicle type which made even a GS seem large was the FS class comprising, initially, 20 minibuses. These were based on the Ford Transit van chassis with a 16-seat body by Strachans. The W9 became London's first minibus service, being introduced on 9 September 1972, and three further routes quickly followed. This photograph taken in autumn 1972 depicts FS 4 at Southgate station. These minibuses were victims of their own success because it became necessary to replace them with larger vehicles on these routes and FS 4 spent nearly four years in store before being withdrawn in July 1979 and sold. As a stop-gap pending the arrival of FS 17 in late 1972 LT hired Strachans' demonstrator which resulted in the unusual sight of a blue bus working the cross-Hampstead C11 route. The minibus is seen here at Archway terminus in the company of RM 579. *Harry Luff/Online Transport Archive); C. Carter/Online Transport Archive*

LEFT AND BELOW LEFT
RLH 2 and RM 1141 stand outside Staines West station, terminus of the railway branch from West Drayton which closed to passengers in 1965. The station building is in its second incarnation, having started life as a private house. Back in 1885, the railway construction company was running short of money and could not afford to build a new station building. The villa/station now survives as prestigious offices. RLH 2, dating from 1950, was withdrawn in 1964, sold to Samuel Ledgard of Leeds and then exported to the USA in 1968. RM 1141 entered service in 1962 and was withdrawn in 1993, only to be scrapped. The second view depicts RLH 54 and shows the vehicle soon after it arrived at Dalston garage for the 178 service in May 1959. It has yet to be fitted with flashing trafficators and has lost a rear wheel disc. Withdrawn in April 1971, RLH 54 was exported to Belgium. *Blake Paterson; Julian Thompson/Online Transport Archive*

We shall never know why, in this spring 1968 view, Camberwell's RT 2493 seems to be parked in the middle of the road at Russell Square with a police car standing behind! The bus is working route 77C which, at the time, ran between Kings Cross and Raynes Park on Saturdays and Sundays. The service was fully converted to RM operation in December 1973, two years after RT 2493 had been consigned to the scrapyard. *Derek Norman/Online Transport Archive*

LEFT Here is a bus promoting trams, on advertising panels at the front and on the side! Photographed at the Parliament Hill Fields terminus at the top end of Highgate Road in summer 1968, RM 1522 carries an early RM production body (as originally fitted to RMs 5-253 which it received on overhaul in February 1968. Withdrawn in July 1984, the vehicle was exported to Germany and was later sold to a buyer in Yugoslavia. *Harry Luff/Online Transport Archive*

LEFT One reason for FRMs never going into production was that FRM 1's arrival coincided with the aftermath of AEC being taken over by Leyland which saw this type of Routemaster as an unwelcome competitor to its Atlanteans. LT took delivery of 50 of the latter buses, designated XA, in 1966 but they turned out to be somewhat unreliable and were exported to Hong Kong in 1973 where they operated until 1980. XA 40 is seen at West Croydon bus station on an Express working in summer 1971. *Harry Luff/Online Transport Archive*

ABOVE A BEA Regal IV coach, NLP 646, leaves the Waterloo Air Terminal (a former 1951 Festival of Britain building) for London Airport (Heathrow) just before the replacement termina at Cromwell Road (built over the Cromwell Curve District Line/ Circle Line junction) opened on 6 October 1957. At that point, garaging/maintenance of the airline coaches transferred from LT's Victoria (Gillingham Street) garage to Shepherds Bush garage. The coach dates from 1953 and carries the original ivory and grey livery (not ivory and blue, as sometimes erroneously portrayed). The airline service ceased on 30 March 1979. *Julian Thompson/Online Transport Archive*

FACING PAGE TOP This Strachans-bodied AEC Merlin, XMS 4 (later to become MB 4 and then MBS 4), entered service on the first "standee" service, route 500, inaugurated on 18 April 1966, and is pictured here on 11 April 1968 in Park Lane. XMS 4 was sold for scrap in November 1979 whereas RM 48, speeding past the Merlin, was more fortunate. Sold to Clydeside Scottish in August 1986 and re-registered, it was later exported to France, becoming a restaurant. *Marcus Eavis/Online Transport Archive*

FACING PAGE BOTTOM RM 2110 overtakes ex-Tilling ST 922 in Whitehall. This open-staircase veteran was a familiar sight on London streets for many years operating Vintage route 100 which was introduced in 1972, when this photograph was taken. The bus has had a fascinating career, entering service at Tilling's Catford (TL) garage in November 1930 and being acquired by LT in October 1933. It was initially withdrawn in 1939, immediately

re-instated and then loaned to Midland Red in December 1941. The bus returned to LT in October 1944 and was sent to Putney garage (AF), from where it was withdrawn in December 1946. ST 922 was then converted into a staff canteen, becoming 693J, until sold by LT to British Road Services in May 1955. Subsequently rescued from a scrapyard, it now belongs to the LBPT. *R. W. A. Jones/Online Transport Archive*

ABOVE Possibly the most attractive livery for the production Merlins was LT Lincoln green, as illustrated by MBS 437 in Reigate in June 1969. The bus has just climbed up Bell Street, past the garage of the erstwhile East Surrey Traction Company and its offices on the corner of Lesbourne Road in which the magnificent Reigate bus garage (part of which survives today) was situated, together with the headquarters of LT's Country Bus & Coach department. *Michael Harries/Author's collection*

All-over advertising was very much in vogue in early 1974 when this photograph was taken. Twenty-seven LT Routemasters were so treated (some may say disfigured) between 1969 and 1976, with RML 2280, seen here at Kensal Rise, suffering twice. This lengthened RM entered service in October 1965 at Godstone garage in red livery (on short-term loan to the Country Area) and was painted with all-over advertising for Hanimex in March 1973, this being changed to Myson's livery seven months later. Repainted red in January 1976, RML 2280 remained in London service until withdrawal in October 2005. The vehicle is still going strong, operated by Wilfreda Beehive, a South Yorkshire coach operator. *C. Carter/Online Transport Archive*

In dire need of a roof repaint which it would never receive with only two months of service remaining before withdrawal, RT 789 pulls out of Westbury Avenue to terminate across the road at Turnpike Lane underground station in September 1974. Enfield would continue to provide RTs for route 217 through to 20 August 1977, after which conversion to DMS operation took place. Prior to 19 May 1954 this route had been numbered 144A. RT 789 had entered service in August 1948 carrying a Park Royal roofbox body and received the Weymann body depicted here at overhaul in November 1967. On withdrawal, the vehicle was sold for scrap.

Derek Norman/Online Transport Archive

In 1965, 43 long double-deck coaches were produced for Green Line services, providing speed and comfort, but sadly to a rapidly decreasing clientele. Dunton Green's RCL 2235 displays its uncluttered image at Victoria in spring 1968 but would shortly receive a repaint and lose its light green window surrounds. RCLs had replaced unreliable RC coaches on route 705 in December 1967 but were themselves displaced by RP coaches in March 1972, whereupon this vehicle was downgraded to operate as a bus. Repurchased from London Country by LT in 1977, RCL 2235 was converted to normal bus configuration in 1980 for route 149 and was given a convertible open-top roof in 1990 for use on the Original London Transport Sightseeing Tour. *Derek Norman/Online Transport Archive*

A freshly painted RT dating from 1949 passes a 1932 Austin 7 as it speeds along the Bath Road (A4) between Cranford and Harlington Corner (alongside Heathrow Airport). However, this is no period shot, the picture being taken in the final year covered by this book when an RT recertification programme was under way due to the unreliability of various more modern types. The bus depicted here, RT 1160, which originally carried a Saunders roofbox body, is working from Shepherds Bush garage on route 105 but wrongly shows a via blind for route 88! The bus remained in use until 1977 when it was sold for scrap. The same fate might have befallen the Austin 7, an early version of the 1933/34 model, had it not been bought by the author for £5 in 1965. The car remains largely unrestored but is still in regular use. *Author*

ABOVE The last survivors of LT's 131-strong TD class of standard provincial Leyland Tiger PS1s supplied to the Central Area operated from Edgware garage, working route 240A until 9 October 1962, after which they were replaced by RFs. This view from the pedestrian steps leading to the Watford Way overbridge shows TD 99 proceeding along Bunns Lane on its way from Mill Hill East station to Edgware station. Four TDs survive, all being the later Mann Egerton-bodied vehicles such as TD 99, but this one, sold to a contractor in 1963, was scrapped following an accident in 1967. *Geoff Morant*

FACING PAGE TOP In May 1968, RF 617 negotiates the A25 roundabout in Dorking, having just left Dorking railway station for the village of Holmbury St Mary on route 412. RF 617 was one of a few RFs which had the distinction of operating a Central

Area service while still in green livery. In January 1969, the bus was transferred to Muswell Hill garage to work route 210 and was not repainted red until June 1969. It remained at that garage until September 1971, ending its operational life at Hounslow garage from where it was withdrawn in January 1977. *Michael Harries/Author's collection*

FACING PAGE BOTTOM RT 4555, which appears to be working on route 69A but is in fact on route 169A (as shown on the canopy blind), stands at Fullwell Cross, Barkingside, on 8 August 1973. This was a relatively short-lived service, being introduced on 19 August 1959 and withdrawn on 19 March 1977. It was RT-operated throughout, though not exclusively, as RTLs and RMLs ran alongside the RTs at various times. *Author's collection*

LEFT AND BELOW In London Country's early days the company was desperately short of operational vehicles and sought help from LT, which was only too glad to hire out some of its AEC Merlin single-deck buses to augment London Country's own Merlin fleet. These views dating from summer 1974 show MB 29 in the company of Routemasters at Crawley bus station and MB 128 in the rural surroundings of Shere. MB 29 had originally been a Red Arrow bus (MBA 29) and ended up being exported to Mauritius in 1977. *Author's collection; Michael Harries/ Author's collection*

ABOVE AND LEFT Over the years, Horse Guards Parade has hosted many different types of event, such as Olympic beach volleyball and Trooping the Colour. This view dating from 21 July 1956 depicts the London General Omnibus Company (LGOC) Centenary Bus Display held at this famous site. The event provided LT with an opportunity to show off the first example of its new bus type, RM 1, which features in the background of both views.
Neil Davenport

FACING PAGE TOP AND BOTTOM Here is an LT-liveried Routemaster working route 27 on 3 November 1962, but you won't find the buildings in the background, nor the tram lines, anywhere between Highgate and Teddington! This is RMF 1254 again, but working Liverpool Corporation's route 27 when it was on trial in that city for four weeks in the vain hope that it would attract orders for this type. The visit took place within days of its delivery to LT on 19 October 1962 following its display on the Park Royal stand at the Commercial Motor Show at Earl's Court. RMF 1254 made other demonstration visits but only two operators were enticed, BEA (see title page and pages 68/69)

and, more surprisingly, Northern General, to which RMF 1254 was sold after it was delicensed by LT on 24 October 1966. *Both: C.Carter/Online Transport Archive*

ABOVE Brand new DMS 410 from Battersea garage reaches the top of Replingham Road at its junction with Wimbledon Park Road, opposite Southfields station, in July 1972. The vehicle had a surprisingly long life for a DMS, being sold for further use and not broken up until 2007. Lasting only ten years with LT, it was lucky not to have been scrapped in 1982, a fate that befell several class members around that time. *C. Carter/Online Transport Archive*

How appropriate to finish a book with the back of a bus! In February 1974, RML 2560 displays its all-over advertising livery for Ladbrokes, the bookmakers, at the East Ham terminus of route 15 outside Central Park, Rancliffe Road. This vehicle entered service at Willesden garage in October 1966 and spent a year advertising Ladbrokes between October 1973 and October 1974, before reverting to red livery. Its London career ended when it was sold in March 2004 and it is currently used as a tour bus in Belfast. Route 15 still operates with traditional Routemasters on a central section between Tower Hill and Trafalgar Square, where it meets the other Routemaster service, a central section of the 9, giving an illusion that London is still running many of these iconic buses.

C. Carter/Online Transport Archive